This book is an unabridged reprint of the first English translation published by Robert Clarke & Co. in 1880. First edition published in 1860.

Typeset and republished by Michael W. Gioffredi. Copyright 2019. MichaelGioffredi.com/5mcp

ISBN-13: 978-1-6720-0305-6

ISBN-10: 1-6720-0305-9

2 4 6 8 10 9 7 5 3

CHARCOAL DRAWING

WITHOUT A MASTER

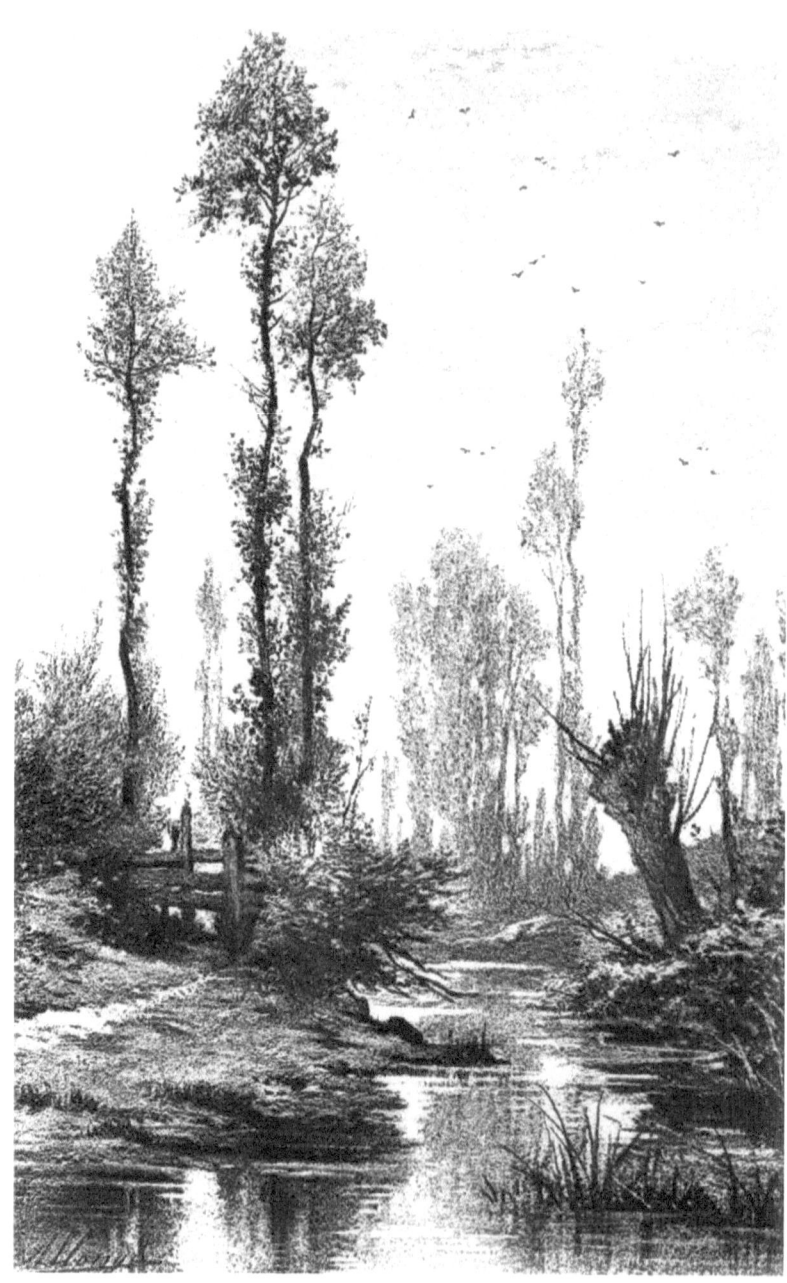

KARL ROBERT—LE FUSAIN

––––––

CHARCOAL DRAWING

WITHOUT A MASTER

A COMPLETE PRACTICAL TREATISE ON LANDSCAPE
DRAWING IN CHARCOAL

FOLLOWED BY LESSONS ON

STUDIES AFTER ALLONGÉ

TRANSLATED FROM THE FOURTH EDITION, BY

ELIZABETH HAVEN APPLETON

––––––

1880

TRANSLATOR'S PREFACE.

It is undeniable that he is the best translator who can transmute the spirit of one language into that of another. To translate properly is to clothe the ideas of a foreign author with a garment of our native words which shall fit them as well as did their original robe ; to give the idiom of one language by its corresponding idiom in another ; not simply to change the French word into an English one. It is the spirit and not the letter that is asked for by the reader.

But true as these rules may be when we judge of translations of purely literary works, —history, belles lettres, etc.—they need to be applied with discretion to translations of scientific works or of technical treatises like this before us. There, exactness is more needed than elegant and idiomatic English.

If, in the chapters on the Material of the Atelier and in the Lessons from the Plates, I have sacrificed the style to a careful and close rendering of the words of Robert, I am sure that the student who makes a practical use of this book will thank me for the sacrifice.　　　　E. H. A.

PREFACE.

Charcoal Drawing is certainly the most rapid, convenient and agreeable method of work for artists, and especially for amateurs, who desire to bring back from a journey or an excursion any notes of the impression produced upon them by the scenes they have passed through, or of the numerous pictorial effects which nature has presented to them.

The use of charcoal for landscape drawing is only of a few years' standing, but it has rapidly become popular, because, while it does not exact much study, it gives prompt and satisfactory results. For this reason we have thought it might be useful to amateurs

to have a practical treatise upon the different ways of executing this new kind of drawing.

Already several very interesting pamphlets, written on this subject, have initiated
the world into this manner of interpreting
nature. But most of these works have either
been incomplete or have treated their subject
simply from the point of view of the author,
generally an artist; consequently they are
without those simple explanations which a
student needs—not from any want of knowledge in the author, but, on the contrary, because, being an artist, he has forgotten the
difficulties which beset a beginner. Few
Artists would consent to undertake a work
which, to be really useful, must be thoroughly
practical and on a level with the student.

In the treatise which we submit to our
readers, they may see that we have made
every effort to be as clear as possible; we
have not been afraid to enter into the sim-

plest details, even at the risk of being charged with puerility ; for we are convinced, from our constant intercourse with amateurs and students, that it is precisely that very information which no one thinks of giving, because it appears so simple, that is really the most needful to persons pursuing any study whatever without the help of a master.

CHARCOAL DRAWING.

THE ORIGIN OF CHARCOAL DRAWING.

CHARCOAL DRAWING AS APPLIED TO THE HUMAN FIGURE.

It does not appear, from the examination of the cartoons in the Museum of the Louvre, that the ancient painters knew any thing of Charcoal Drawing. The honor derived from its use belongs entirely to modern artists; nor is this surprising, since, as we shall see further, the very invention of charcoal crayons is recent.

The first application of Charcoal Drawing

was to the human figure. Certain painters made use of it, at first, in the studies for their pictures.

The School of Fine Arts (L'Ecole des Beaux-Arts) admitted it at once for the sketches submitted to the Academy; and, little by little, artists carried their charcoal drawings farther than mere sketches; for, as they found that this new kind of crayon gave to their work a stronger character than those employed before, they adopted it for the entire picture.

The employment of the charcoal crayon dates from the years 1847 and 1848, when one of the greatest French historical painters, Adolphe Ivon,* gave his earliest studies to the

---

* Adolphe Ivon, French painter, born at Eschevillor (Moselle), 1817, pupil of Paul Delaroche, made, in 1843, a journey to Eusaia, whence he brought back a series of studies, which ho made use of for the beautiful drawings exhibited at the Exposition of 1847, and at that of 1848. He sent out, next, the "Battle of Kouli-

public ; studies, where, by the aid of charcoal crayon, heightened sometimes by water color or by oil, he succeeded in obtaining those brilliant and dramatic effects which placed him immediately in the front rank of modern artists. The Museum of Havre possesses a complete example of his finest composition in his "Seven Cardinal Sins."

Later, he succeeded in reproducing, in this

kowo," in 1850; "Marshal Ney encouraging the Arriere Guard" (the Retreat from Russia), in 1855; "The Seven Capital Sins," also in 1855; "The Taking of Malakoff," 1857; "The Gorge of Malakoff," 1858; "The Fortifications of Mahikoff," 1859; and, last, "The Independence of the United States of America," in 1870. Tills last picture, much criticised, is none the less a grand page in history, where can be found the imprint of strong talent joined to learned composition. M. Ivon obtained a first medal in 1848, a second medal in 1855, the grand medal of honor in 1857, a second medal at the Universal Exposition of 1866. Named Chevalier the Legion of Honor in 1855, he was promoted to the grade of officer in 1867.

manner, certain souvenirs of Russia, where he executed, after nature, a series of studies which, to-day, have become very valuable. He proved also, by drawings made to illustrate some works on art and on history, especially by his illustrations of the History of Russia, that this kind of design would take the place, even for book illustrations, of almost all the processes employed before, because of its wonderful power of giving effect to military or to historical scenes.

In our time, Charcoal Drawing has been followed by genre painters. In the first rank among them we would mention E. Bayard, whose reputation has been established by his souvenirs of that year so fatal to us, 1870-71, and by his charming compositions, *"Before"* and *"After the War."* M. Gelibert has also employed charcoal with success and, by its use, has given a still greater originality to his drawings of animals and to his hunting scenes.

Painters on glass have made use of charcoal, for a long time, for their designs or patterns for their work, on account of the facility of treating rapidly the shadows of drapery or of architecture offered them by the charcoal crayon; but the outlines are always traced by the black crayon or the lithographic pencil, which gives them a certain required sharpness.

The names which we have cited prove that Charcoal Drawing lends itself easily to any artistic reproductions, that it can reach up to high art as well as it can throw off a mere fantasy.

But it excels above all in landscape, as we hope to prove; and it is for this reason that this branch of art has taken so firm a position and has spread itself so widely and rapidly among amateurs.

OF CHARCOAL DRAWING AS APPLIED TO LANDSCAPE.

ALLONGÉ, APPIAN, BELLEL, LALANNE, REYÉ.

As soon as the first start was given to Charcoal Drawing, the landscape painters profited most by it. Even Decamps made use of it; by the medium of Charcoal Drawing he gave those lovely inspirations and that severe style which made such an impression on the artistic world. Troyon, Paul Huett and others followed in this new path,—and now there is not a landscape painter who does not put a package of charcoal crayons with his working materials when he starts on an excursion. And he is right. This means of rendering in a few minutes, a view, an effect, has a charm for the landscape painter, who can thus bring bixck, from even a short journey, a collection of varied studies, each one bearing the impress of nature. Moreover, the new material aids the artist in his progress by giving a variety to his work which can never be attained by those who do not make use of it.

Still, we do not mean to say that Charcoal Drawing should ever take the place of painting; we mean, only, that the study of it ought to precede the use of color, and we are ready to affirm that every artist who gives his attention to that study will, thereby, strengthen his talent.

As to the superiority of Charcoal Drawing over all other means of rendering landscape, painting excepted, we shall not here undertake to demonstrate it. M. Allongé, in his book, which can be considered as the "Esthetics of Charcoal," has well shown that superiority for a broad interpretation of nature, and he brings out the full value of the charcoal crayon, when he compares it with the black-lead pencil, which is thin and harsh even in rendering the smallest effects.

To appreciate the numberless resources which the use of charcoal offers, we have only to look at the works of the masters who have brought it to perfection, and to study them carefully. Messieurs Allongé, Appian, Bellet, Lalanne, each in a different style, have arrived at the most complete results. Bellet, the eldest, seems to be the one who has made the fewest concessions to modem taste. His fine and severe compositions come evidently from classic models. We feel there an innovation only in the material employed; the mode of employment remains the same, the black crayon would give the same effects. The other masters, on the contrary, have changed, if I may so express myself, the general tone of their works: if the material is new, the manner of working it is so likewise.

And all these artistically capricious methods of working in charcoal are the very cause of the variety we find in it.

Adolphe Appian, of Lyons,* has joined figure to landscape, with a wonderful harmony. Every one can judge of his success at the Luxembourg Museum, where one of his finest compositions, "The Return from the Fields," was placed some years ago. The landscape, perhaps sacrificed a little to the figure, is not, for that, the less broadly treated ; but how fine this figure is, how full of a charming and natural grace ! Certainly this

---

* Adolphe Appian, born at Lyons, pupil of L'Ecole des Beaux-Arts in that city, and of Corot and Daubigny, exhibited for the first time a design in charcoal, in 1855, and was soon publicly noticed. He put out, successively, very beautiful charcoal drawings of the borders of the Isère, of the valley of Optorez, of the environs of Nice, etc. This artist obtained a medal in Paris, in 1868, at Eochelle, at Pengireaux, at Lyons, etc., and recently, in Vienna, two gold medals, in the departments of painting and of etching.

is not the peasant woman of our modern real-
ists. The artist has put his heart in it, and,
under this rustic dress, it is rather the mother
than the peasant woman that he has tried to
make us admire. Unhappily, the works of
this master are not yet much known in Paris ;
the people of Lyons, who admire him, have
monopolized him almost entirely, and then
Charcoal Drawing gains a footing in Paris
only little by little, thanks to the efforts of
some merchants connected with artists.* Here
we should like to relate an anecdote, which
proves the want of intelligence of those people who are in the best position to make a
new talent known to the world.

M. Appian, as modest as he is full of
talent, wished, some time ago, to let himself

---

* We mention especially M. Dangleterre, picture
framer, Rue do Seine, who, in 1855, divined, from the
early works of M. Allongé, what that young artist
would become ; and, in the same way, M. Berville saw
the future merit of Maxime Lalanne.

be known in Paris as an artist in charcoal;
his merit as a painter being already established, as it had brought him a medal at the
Exposition. He called the attention of the
best known picture dealer in Paris to the
study of Charcoal Drawing; and, on offering
to place one of his drawings in his shop, obtained the privilege as a great favor. A short
time afterward, he found this very drawing in
a loft, the glass which covered it broken, the
drawing in a pitiable state. Then he deter-
mined never to make the trial again. We
hope, however, that the eminent artist will re-
consider this decision, which is to be regretted
by every lover of Charcoal Drawing.

Maxime Lalanne is one of those landscape artists who strike at first sight by their
originality. What does he need to make a
charcoal sketch? A corner, an old street,
a chateau in ruins. Sober in details, he
treats Charcoal Drawing a little too much like

etching, in which he excels, but what poetry,
what perfect taste in his choice of a subject !
"Allongé,"* said once F. Petit, the learned

* Auguste Allonge, born in Paris in 1833, papil of
L'Ecole des Beaux-Arts, rewarded by a medal in the
School, in 1853 ; crowned by the Academy, in 1854 ; ex-
hibiting, for the first time, at the Universal Exposition
of 1858, a large design, "Souvenir of the "Gorge-aux-
Loups ;" and after this, every year, paintings and drawings. The best known are "The Ponds of Péray,"
charcoal ; "Sheep in the Island of Creteil," a painting ;
"The Fountain of Sainte-Barbe" (Morbihan), charcoal ; "The Sea at Portrieux ;" "The Willow Thicket
Inundated," 1866, a charcoal drawing, bought by M.
Prince Stirbey ; "The Valley of Gouët," 1868, painting ; "The Beach at Villers," painting ; "The Footpath
to the Fountain" (Villers), charcoal, 1869 ; "October in
the Forest," painting ; "The Valley of Hygères," charcoal, 1870 ; "View of the City of Puy," painting,
bought by the government ; "Solitude," charcoal, 1872 ;
the Salon of 1873, and the Exposition in Vienna, 1873,
belonging to M. Delaporte, of St. Quentin ; "L'Hyére
à Crosne," painting ; "The Pool," a charcoal drawing,
bought by M. the Count of Audiffret. And, at the last

artistic expert, "Allongé is Charcoal Drawing, and Charcoal Drawing is simply Allongé." Indeed, it would seem that this master has given every effect possible to his material. Let him treat a woodland scene, the banks of a river, a group of willows, the open country, mountains or sea, we feel always the artist, born painter, who paints by the help of a single color. But what myriads of tones in this blackness of charcoal! What a just feeling of values, what a charm in that perspective full of light, in those forms, always elegant and graceful!

To conclude, amateurs may see now, at Messieurs Goupil, Boulevard Montmartre, a new style of Charcoal Drawing; I mean the

Salon, "The Sea," a picture, bought by the govern-ment; "A Farm of Normandy," charcoal, bought by M. Colas. Since he gained his medal at L'Ecole dos Beaux-Arts, M. Allongé has obtained a large number of prizes; at Paris, in 1866, for Fine Arts applied to Industry, the first gold medal, at Havre, La Rochelle, Bourges, etc.

works of M. Reyé. Although we are not
very partial to his manner of interpreting
nature by means of an absolute white and
an intense black, applied to a paper first
covered with gum and spread with white
lead, yet we recognize the true talent there
to be taken into account, and we see that,
if the artist would conform to modern tastes
and ideas, he would be very near taking
rank as a master. It is above all in half
tints and distant planes that Charcoal Drawing has its great charm; thus any one who
neglects these, becomes harsh. M. Reyé is
a pupil of Calame and he has not yet laid
aside the mantle of his master. Now, Calame, who had a well-deserved success in his
own time, is a little out of fashion in our
day; and this is not surprising, landscape
painting having made considerable progress
in fifty years. We hope that M. Reyé will
pardon us our frankness, but if we permit
ourselves to judge in this way his original

works, it is because we are convinced that the public may discuss his talent to-day, and even criticise it, only to admire it to-morrow without restriction.

Considered from the amateur's point of view, Charcoal Drawing is the only study that can give a serious result to amateur work; and if every father of a family understood what resources were to be found against idleness in developing in young people a taste for drawing by this simple means, there soon would not be a man having received a certain amount of education, who would not know how to employ his leisure agreeably in the country, or even in a city, where every one would take pleasure in passing his evenings in his own family, seated before his easel.

We go out of our subject, it is true, but we have always regretted that in our schools of art the study of landscape is set aside. Certainly we do not wish to deny the utility of academic studies, but out of the hundred young men who follow a course of design, ten or twenty, perhaps, profit really by the instruction which is given, them; the others, on the contrary, taking for excuse their want of taste, become discouraged and make no progress. This would never happen if the study of landscape was admitted; then, on leaving the school, loving an art in which they had acquired a certain facility, they would devote their leisure to it.

THE FURNITURE OF THE ATELIER.

FURNITURE OF THE ATELIER.

If it has passed into a proverb that he is a bad workman who complains of his tools, it is certain that to have good ones simplifies work, renders it more agreeable and brings a more satisfactory result. Therefore we shall not be afraid of being too diffuse in this chapter, or of entering into the smallest details concerning the different accessories necessary to the study of Charcoal Drawing. Whether you are an artist by pro-

(33)

fession or are only a lover of sketching, surround yourself with every thing that can be useful to you, and, believe the words of experience, you will gain a serious advantage from this precaution.

The Easel.

The furniture of an atelier is composed, first, of an easel; and we believe, if one does much work, it will be best to procure a mechanical easel, called the Easel Bonhomme, because the common easels with three feet, very convenient for small drawings, will not support the frame sufficiently if you are working upon a design larger than the board called the supporter; for then there will be constantly a movement from right to left and from left to right, under the pressure

of the hand during the work. If you can
not obtain an easel Bonhomme, you may
make use of the common eaisel with three
feet, which is much less costly and almost
as convenient. And you can even obviate
the inconvenience of which we spoke above,
by placing at the height of about twenty-two
inches on the movable supporter when it is
arranged for the hand in working seated, a
cross-piece of wood, fixed by nails or move-
able by the help of screws held by small
nuts ; a cross-piece, which, being of the same
size as the supporter, will very easily hold
the frame. This will not be very agreeable
to the sight, but it will render the same service as the mechanical easel. If you prefer
the latter, take one with a fixed stand, less
easily broken than a sliding stand. We say
nothing of the easels provided with pulleys ;
they are seldom used now, on account of the
difficulty, when the supporting board is once

raised, of drawing it down at need without shaking it.

As to the easel for holding the model, with a single stand and cross feet, it is, in our opinion, altogether useless, seeing that, by the help of a hook fixed at the top of the easel on which you are working, you can always hang up your model, which will be supported by the very frame on which you are making your copy. If the model is too large to permit this arrangement, you can place it on a chair, on a table easel or on a common one ; but in no case should you make use of the model-bearing easel, which is never firm enough to hold a large drawing, and which the least touch would shake.

The Frame.

In the atelier, a frame is the best thing on which to stretch your paper, it is also the cheapest, and indeed it is the only thing which stretches well and which offers a proper resistance. The frame ought to be made like those which you employ for canvas, but it need not be furnished with braces. And, moreover, it will be found convenient to attach* to it, at the middle of the back, a cross-piece of wood, which, when the drawing is finished, will permit you to hold it easily in order to set it.

* We say "attach," because if you insert the cross-piece into the frame, as you do in those used for canvas, you will find it troublesome to set the drawing, the brush not passing easily under the bar.

You must not be discouraged if, the first time you stretch your paper, the result is not perfect. It is a matter of habit, and we assure you that, if you conform exactly to the instructions which we give you here, you will succeed in stretching your paper rapidly, without wrinkles, which never can be done with the ordinary stretcher.

To stretch your paper, after having cut it large enough to overlap the frame about an inch and a half on each side, you lay it on a table, the right side or, better, the grain of the paper, against the table; then, by the help of a little sponge, you moisten the wrong side from one end to the other. The paper thoroughly moistened, you lay the frame upon it and fasten one of the sides with tacks, one in the middle and one at each end. This done, you turn your frame, and repeat the same operation for the opposite side, then go on in the same way for the other two sides, taking care to press down the corners of the paper in drawing them a little over the edge of the frame. This work ought to be done as rapidly as possible. When the paper is thus held at each of the four sides by the three tacks, you should place between them as many other nails as you think needed, according to the size of the paper.

To stretch a paper well, put tacks at distances of about an inch and a half and, whilst you are putting them in, draw the paper, so as to stretch it as much as possible while it is moist, but do this gently, that it may not tear under your hands. This work finished, let the paper dry at the temperature of the weather; at the end of a half hour in winter and a quarter of an hour in summer, it will be as well stretched as a painting canvas. In winter you must be very careful not to dry it before the fire for, in that case, the paper will wrinkle at a lower temperature and become loosened while you are working at it.

The Stretcher.

An instrument composed of two frames shut, one into the other, or placed and held, one above the other, by means of brads and clasps ; this is used very commonly for stretching the paper in Charcoal Drawing. For the first kind of stretcher, you need only place the moistened paper over the larger frame, then, placing the second frame upon the first, press it until you close the machine. For the second kind of stretcher, the use of it is still more simple ; you place the paper very evenly between the two frames and fold them at once, one over the other. This stretcher is convenient for out-of-door sketching, since you do not need all the apparatus of the frame, nails, hammer, etc., but it is very inferior for

work in the atelier. The stretcher with
clasps, drawing horizontally upon the paper,
tears it easily when it dries and stretches.
The other instrument, drawing the paper by
means of a ledge which enters one of the
frames from the other, tears it very easily
also, especially in the corners. But there is a
third stretcher which combines all the desired
conditions. It is composed of two frames
which, laid over each other, shut together by
means of an interior groove. Moreover, it is
improved by a frame covered with linen or
muslin, which permits you to carry the drawing, without injury, before it is set. In this
way, you may give several days to a drawing from nature. This stretcher has not the
fault of the first mentioned, because the corners are free, and it does not tear the paper,
like the second, because the tension is not
horizontal. But, to be absolutely perfect, this
machine needs such care in its construction.

that the price is necessarily too high to justify any merchant in keeping it on hand.

The Charcoal Crayons.*

You can certainly draw with all kinds of charcoal crayons; nevertheless, it is well to have, for landscape drawing in charcoal, those of a superior quality. The common crayon used in sketching, ought to be rejected, for it is better to employ, for the sketch, the same crayon which is used to finish the drawing. The artists' charcoal crayon, marked R. G. M., is certainly the best. It is the natural wood,

---

* Fasain, s. m. Term of botany. A shrub which grows naturally along hedges, whose wood serves to make distaffs, spindles, earding needles, etc.; or, reduced to charcoal, is employed to draw light sketches. Spindle-tree or Prickwood (*Euonymus*). — *Dictionary of the Academy.*

and simply charred with care ; unctious and pleasant to handle, it gives the most intense blacks and, at the same time, the softest grays for the background and the more distant planes, when you work it down with a stomp. For details and fine branches it is well to make use of a crayon made from the little shrub called mignonette,* which, harder than the other, is quite as black and does not crumble from the pressure of the hand. It can be cut to as fine a point as possible, so that you can render with it the most tender twigs and the lightest details.

The Venitian charcoal crayon is not bad, but it is no better than the R. G. M., and it costs much more. There is also the charcoal crayon made from the broom handle ;† a kind of hard wood, thick as a candle, which, cut

* A variety of *Resida*, with a woody stem, larger than the mignonette cultivated here.

† Rather indefinite, as we do not know from what kind of wood broom handles are made in France.

flat, serves well for skies, and for even tints on a broad surface.

But there is a kind of crayon called soaked (*trempé*) which you must never use. These crayons, which are nothing but common charcoal dipped into a composition making a black liquid, are far from having the worth of the natural crayon. Dry and hard, they interfere continually with good work and are, at the very best, only fit for sketches. I know that the paper in which they are wrapped is a great attraction; but, in this case, contrary to the proverb, the flag does not cover the merchandise.

We do not approve of vigorous retouches by the aid of the black or lithographic crayon. They take from the Charcoal Drawing the softness which characterizes it; but still there are some cases where a sharp touch is useful. The crayon H. Conte is, then, the best to employ. Pulverized charcoal is now used, sometimes, for skies, background and retouches.

The Paper.

In the two most interesting and most practical pamphlets which have been written on
Charcoal Drawing, those of Lalanne and of
Allongé, there is such a direct opposition in
the recommendations of the paper to be employed, that we will quote the two para-
graphs and give afterward our own opinion
on the subject, specifying the manner in
which the student may use with advantage
either kind of paper.

M. Lalanne says, "If the paper has a
certain roughness, like that of grained paper,
it will catch the friable particles of the charcoal and, whatever be the subject you wish to
treat, you will do well, after having cut your
crayon, to pass a general tone over every

thing, which will give, as it were, a com-
mencement of values. You will not have to
work afterwards on a white surface, but upon a
preparatory background already established.
This value may be modified according to the
different planes of the subject." In Allongé
we find, on the contrary, "What forces me to
condemn those papers which have too rough a
grain, or any regular divisions, is that I find
it absolutely necessary, for the background, to
be able to lighten the tone, in order to render
it more delicate, in accordance with its plane,
however vigorous it may be as a tone. The
same is true in the representation of water.
Now, if the grain of the paper gives, in the
background, the same effects as in the foreground, it forces you to leave, in your work,
sharp, white points in every light, however
much these lights may differ the one from
the other ; you will have neither planes nor
values, for this white grain will render the
yellow as well as the green, the dull tones as

well as the brilliant ones, and the pictorial
aspects of your work will disappear."

This objection to the employment of rough
paper appears to us very just; for, putting
aside the fact that it is very difficult, in pre-
paring a general tone as M. Lalanne directs,
to obtain, with such paper, a fine, even and
every-where equal tone where the grain shall
not appear, we meet, in using it, another
obstacle. Between the roughnesses which
catch the crayon, we see the tint of the paper itself; and this, far from giving a fresh
and distant tone, leads the pupil to make
drawings in which the sky and the water are
unsteady, and where the ground itself wants
solidity. Moreover, this paper is so light in
its quality that it is difficult to use it on the
frame or on the stretcher. It can only be
used on blocks or on a pasteboard as it is prepared for the Academy; this can never give
the delicacy of paper that is stretched.

But still, we must not condemn this rough

paper entirely : in the first place, because M.
Lalanne, making use of it with his talent, has
really obtained the result of which he speaks ;
and secondly, because we believe that, in certain cases, it facilitates execution, especially
when you wish to reproduce ruins, villages, old
picturesque streets and buildings in fact.
But we must proscribe this paper on princi-
ple, in all teaching, because in using it the
pupil will have to conquer difficulties which a
good paper does not present. Therefore, we
advise the papers used by M. Allongé and M.
Appian, which are a dull yellow or else white,
with a fine and even grain. With these papers
you can treat every subject, provided you
know how to modify and vary your work according to the nature of the subject you wish
to reproduce.

There is no other special precaution to be
given with regard to the paper, except to keep
it always pure and clean, and, in putting it on
the frame or on the stretcher, to take care not

to moisten the side on which you are going to
draw, as this makes spots which are difficult
to get rid of.

We never employ, and we counsel our
readers against employing, tinted papers. If
you desire to obtain a general yellow tint,
dissolve a little saffron in your white fixative.

Stomps, Spills, Punk, Wadding, Linen and Woolen Rags, Pith of the Elder-Bush, The Employment and the Preservation of Bread-Crumbs.

All these accessories and their manner
of employment have so much importance, in
our opinion, that we can not content ourselves
with simply giving a list of them.

The paper stomp is that most frequently
used. All paper stomps, being made in the
same way, are equally good ; to keep them so,

you have only to press them with care, immediately after your work, to prevent them
from losing their point ; otherwise you can no
longer obtain delicate results—they will be
good for nothing except for flat work.

The flat stomp, called the hare's foot, is
very useful for obtaining a uniform tone on a
broad surface ; you should always use it for
reflections in the water.

Amongst other stomps, those of leather, of
silk, of cork, etc., the leather stomp is the
only one which appears to us of any use in
Charcoal Drawing. It obtains clear tones
and half-tints. It is generally used in broad
tints, which the paper stomp would not make
light enough and which bread-crumb would
make too light.

Spills render nearly the same service as
paper stomps, especially for small surfaces.
They are more supple, more agreeable to handle and, besides, much cheaper. Indeed, you

can make them yourself with gray paper, blotting paper or silk paper.

The Rag.

To pass a general tone over your paper, and take from it the crudeness of the white, and also to obtain sky values, you should generally use the palm of the hand or the four fingers joined, after having laid on, as regularly as possible, the quantity of charcoal necessary to obtain the regular values. But if you want a brilliant and clear sky or transparent and luminous water, the use of a piece of old linen or of old cotton is excellent. You must roll up the rag so that it may present a broad and even surface, then, turning it from the bottom of your paper toward the top, you can spread the charcoal. But, to prevent this

operation from doing harm to the work which
follows it, it must be performed with skill; it
should be done, so to say, at the first trial;
otherwise, if you are obliged to make several
attempts, the charcoal, sinking too much into
the paper, will give a tone either too light or
too dark, according to the quantity first placed
there; and then, even with the help of bread-
crumb, you can never obtain a fresh light nor
a brilliant and lively tone to lighten a cloud
or a sunbeam on the water. To obtain this
same general tone, many persons use glove
kid, punk, wadding, etc. But these are inferior to the rags; they are more difficult to
use, they often make spots or cottony, heavy,
disagreeable skies. You may use them to
mark out the clouds, but not for the tone of
the background or clear sky, which ought
always to be smooth and even. You can obtain this tone only by the aid of the rag. Use,
for that purpose, pulverized charcoal, covering
with it the roll of cloth which we have just

described. This will give a soft and light tone, one on which you then can model your clouds.

The Bread-Crumb.

Carefully crumbled and worked into a flat or pointed lump, it is used, as we know, for the most brilliant lights. You must always use stale, home-made bread ; fresh bread will grease the paper and injure your retouches. To keep your bread-crumb, you must press it into a little metal box, lead or tin, such as are sold for snuff-boxes. In that way, you can keep it two or three days, according to the season. This is a very convenient way of keeping it, especially on excursions ; the box of bread-crumb takes up but little space and yet you can press in enough to serve for several drawings.

The Eraser.

This instrument fills a role important
enough in Charcoal Drawing to make it necessary to choose it with care ; it is used to obtain middle tints in the details of the work,
where the stomp or the spill would not give
enough delicacy of touch. You may use it advantageously for the foliage of trees on the
second plane, and also on the first planes, to
mark out grass, furze and reeds. Let the
eraser be always very sharp, otherwise it will
take off the surface of the paper and, in fixing the drawing, the liquid will make a smutch.
The common eraser, fixed or shutting into its
case by means of a groove, is excellent ; but
what is still better is the eraser called the
scalpel. With the point you can obtain a

great delicacy of touch and with the edge you may work upon broader surfaces than with the common eraser. Moreover, this eraser is more conveniently held between the fingers and allows you to work always in the same direction.

The Fixative.

DIFFERENT WAYS OF FIXING OR SETTING THE CHARCOAL.

Indirect Fixation (the fixative applied to the back of the paper).—The fixing of Charcoal Drawing, when the work is finished, needs very great care. There have been many preparations employed up to this time; but we must confess that none of them give a positively good result. You may suspect quackery in all those inventors who claim complete success on this point. The first fixative employed was that of Durozier, used especially by painters on glass. It sets the drawing well and is well enough for sketches on pasteboard, etc.; but it gives to the paper a very disagreeable yellow tone which destroys its effect; above all, it hurts an effect of light. Moreover, in passing over the paper, it gives a shiny look to the drawing, which takes away the principal charm of Charcoal Drawing, that dead tone which gives its value and its harmony.

The other fixatives, those of M. Rouget, M. Berville, etc., being of nearly the same composition, give about the same result, in spite of the claims of their inventors; but the fixative Meusnier, adopted by Allongé and his pupils, who prefer it to all others, has the advantage of being suitable for direct fixation without the necessity of cleaning the apparatus during the work, a disagreeable operation of which we shall speak presently. As to the manner of fixing the drawing, it is the opinion generally adopted and the only true one, that Charcoal Drawings fixed on the back of the paper, are always the most permanent.* This is besides the most convenient and rapid method. You pour the preparation into a cup or a saucer, and then by the aid of a flat brush, which you will fill with the fixative by dipping it into the liquid, you moisten your drawing on the wrong side, holding the same by the cross piece at the back. When the drawing is well covered with the fixative, you must dry it as rapidly as possible, in the sun in summer, and not far from the fire in winter. The fixative, drying rap-

---

* The superiority of the fixative Measnior is incontestible; its only inconvenience is the strong odor which characterizes it; to avoid this, it will be well to fix your drawing near an open window and to keep the bottle well corked when it is not in use. This fixative can be obtained from any color merchant or dealer in artistic materials.

idly, catches the charcoal dust on the paper, makes it adhere and, so to say, sets it in the drawing. We point out the use of the cup as most economical; but, if you don't care for that, you can pour the liquid on the back of your drawing and spread it every-where, equally, with the brush. But in this way you lose a great deal of your fixative and the drawing is no better set.

Direct Fixation (*the fixative applied to the drawing itself*).—Artists generally use for this purpose, and wrongly, we think, the blowing apparatus Rouget. We regret not to be of the opinion with regard to it of M. Maxime Lalanne, and these are the reasons which make us judge it differently. In the first place, direct fixation is far from giving, instantaneously, the promised result. You must repeat the operation several times and, for this, you must wait each time until the paper dries, to obtain the same permanent setting that you get by indirect fixation.

Then the use of this apparatus is not easy,
because it must be cleaned every time it is
used; otherwise it gets dirty and the capil-
lary tube, which is the base of the invention,
becomes choked up. And, if you blow too
quickly or if you bring the instrument too
near the drawing, the atomization is not
complete—a jet of the liquid may strike the
drawing, dragging along with it the charcoal
and making a smutch impossible to retouch,
and in one minute you may lose the work of
several hours. Lastly, blowing by the mouth
being necessarily irregular, you can never
obtain an absolute regularity of the vapor.
You must give up this instrument above all
in sketching from nature.

It results from what we have just said,
that direct fixation ought never to be employed except when it is indispensable, that
is to say, when you wish to fix a design on
cloth, silk, etc.; for a sketch prepared for
painting or for screens, fans, and the like.

In that case, the best apparatus is that used in medicine for the atomization of mineral waters, obtained by the atomizer of rubber, invented by Galand. We know that this instrument is more expensive than that of Rouget but it is much less fragile, and gives so much better results, that it is good economy to employ it. Then, the wind not being given by the mouth but by two balls pressed alternately, the atomizing tube does not become choked, and thus you avoid the cleaning, a tiresome operation, especially when working from nature.

Material for the Country.

It is well to reduce, as much as possible, your material for out-door work, for you never know, in starting, if the view which charms you will be near home or if you will be ob-

liged to make a long tramp before finding it.
It is a good habit to work on your lap, and
thereby get rid of the field easel, which, in
spite of all the ingenuity of the manufactu-
rers, is always heavy enough to tire you.

But you will do well always to have a camp-
stool, for, in sitting on the ground,* you are
often troubled by the horizon, which then appears above your eye, or by the first planes,
to which you can not give sufficient preponder-
ance. If you wish to make careful studies or
harmonious drawings, it is well to provide
yourself with an umbrella; for, if you are
sketching in the open country in the sun-
shine, no matter what vigor you may give to
your drawing, it will always appear gray; you

* "From time to time, the artist should stoop, to assure himself that the lines of the landscape which he
has found harmonious when viewed standing, will present the same rhythm when he has altered the perspective point of view, by sitting down."—*The Landscape
Artist in the Fields by F. Henriet.*

work it up and you are surprised, on return-
ing to your atelier, to find that you have
made a drawing extremely black, recalling
the touch of the crayons of Conte or of the
lithographic pencil; the planes have no longer
their relative values and your design has the
fault of harshness, an unpardonable fault in
Charcoal Drawing.

As to all those boxes for Charcoal Drawing, made like the field boxes for oil painting,
and in general all apparatus of this sort, be
careful not to embarrass yourself with them.
A few charcoal crayons, a stomp, two or three
spills, the snuff-box with the bread-crumb,
an eraser—all these can be put in your pocket,
and it is just because this mode of drawing is
the least troublesome that it is the most
agreeable. There is only the box for the
frame that appears to us really useful. This
is a sort of open box, which has neither top
nor bottom and in which you can fasten the
frames of stretched paper by means of copper

clamps. Get the lightest boxes possible. By
the help of a little strap on the handle you
can carry the little tin can holding the fixative, and in the same way you can fasten the
camp-stool and the umbrella.

STUDIES AND LESSONS.

STUDY AFTER THE MASTERS.

ON THE CHOICE OP MODELS.

There is a sentence often repeated to those who are beginning the study of drawing or of painting; this is, "Be yourself, try to be original; success lies there." Certainly, when well understood, this is an absolute truth. But it does not therefore follow that it is useless to copy models or that you should work from nature without any previous study.

It is very true that, by dint of labor and

(67)

perseverance, you can reach good results from nature, above all if you are endowed with a special talent for drawing. But this treatise is not written for the few exceptional artists by birth—its object is to be useful to amateurs, not to interest artiste. Therefore we tell the amateur that to begin at once to draw from nature will be a mistake for him. He should subject his hand and his eye to work, less agreeable, it is true, but more useful. By copying you obtain, little by little, a satisfactory knowledge of the means employed in Charcoal Drawing and, from that very knowledge, you will be less embarrassed when you draw from nature. But to make your copying profitable, it must be seriously studied and your models should be chosen with great care.

You should not copy from engravings nor from old lithographs, for, says Allongé, "These landscapes, however well sketched, having the white paper for the sky, whether gray, blue or white, make use of it again for lights on a road, for foliage in sunlight, as well as for the dull tone of tree trunks, the lights of thatch or brick, the bright spots of stone or plaster."

We do not condemn these models altogether; there is good in every thing, but you must know how to profit by it. The student who does not know how to draw and who wishes to succeed in Charcoal Drawing, should work, outside of his special study, on small copies in lead pencil, which will give him facility of hand and render him more skillful when he comes to treat Charcoal. Drawing with delicacy and to give careful details.

You can begin by copying the landscape drawing books, method Cassagne, but only for first models; for this method, excellent for buildings, appears to us defective when you come to trees.

If you are working for Charcoal Drawing,

the particular study of the leaf is not useful ; you should habituate yourself, as much as possible, to treat trees by masses and by effects and not by the detail of the foliage. For this, you may copy some models from the album of Hubert, taking care to add a graded background for the sky.

Lately, many persons have copied in charcoal photographs after nature ; this is very bad. These photographs, made with care and excellent guides for artists, since they give the exact and minute form of the objects reproduced, force the pupil into useless little details and lead him away from a large interpretation of nature. We may affirm this : for the study of Charcoal Drawing there are only two kinds of good models—reproductions of charcoal work by good methods, as we have had lately, such as lithophotography or heliography, or better still in Paris, the Charcoal Drawings themselves, which you can

easily obtain either by hiring them or by sub-
scription.

This want of good models for drawing,
and particularly for Charcoal Drawing, will
soon be supplied, thanks to the intelligent energy of Messrs. Groupil & Co. Foreseeing
the important position which this kind of
artistic work will soon take, this house has
asked of M. Allongé a series of models which
will form a course of landscape drawing.
Nothing can be more practical or more complete than this collection of designs, where it
would seem that the master has surpassed
himself. You will find in this course all the
examples and the teaching which is necessary
for study from nature. All is treated; trees,
first planes, forests, river banks, mountains
and sea-views. And it is to be remarked
that, in this collection, each drawing, taken
separately, forms a real landscape, even in the
first of the series.

There are none of the dry elements and

principles of the old methods. The master has undertaken to demonstrate his principles by charming the student or the amateur ; and, from the opinion of those who have seen the originals, we can say that he has completely attained the end which he proposed to himself.

The reproduction of these Charcoal Drawings is a real marvel. We have shown the proofs to several artists, and we can state that the *fac simile* is so good that almost every one of them has taken the reproduction for a real Charcoal Drawing.

In conclusion, it is evident that this is a great step made in the teaching of drawing, and we hope that this result obtained in the reproduction of Charcoal Drawings, will facilitate the introduction of the study into the public schools.

We advise the amateur to take the drawings of M. Allongé as models and his manner as their method, because his designs are executed in so clear and neat a manner that, by the time you have copied the second drawing, you know the method of the artist. We do not say this because we are a pupil of M. Allongé, on the contrary it was because this was our opinion that we chose him for a master.

When, after some months of study, you have acquired the manner of working, in a word the secret of Charcoal Drawing, you may try it in every way. The drawings of Appian and Lalanne ought to be taken at the end of your studies. The works of these two masters do not present themselves clearly to the mind in the way of execution, and in our opinion you must have all the talent that they possess to arrive at such results by such simple means.

Copies after Painting.

The passage from copying to original work is often difficult, and the student who, by perseverance, has come to be a faithful copyist, does not always succeed in giving a satisfactory work from nature. Thus we believe that it is an excellent transition work to render a few oil paintings into charcoal. If in such a picture the drawing is clear, if the form is easy to reproduce, you must still study for yourself the values which the painter has rendered, values which are the absolute bases of art. Moreover, the execution of painting having nothing in common with the method of Charcoal Drawing, you can profit by your former work, and learn gradually to take advantage of all the methods in your power.

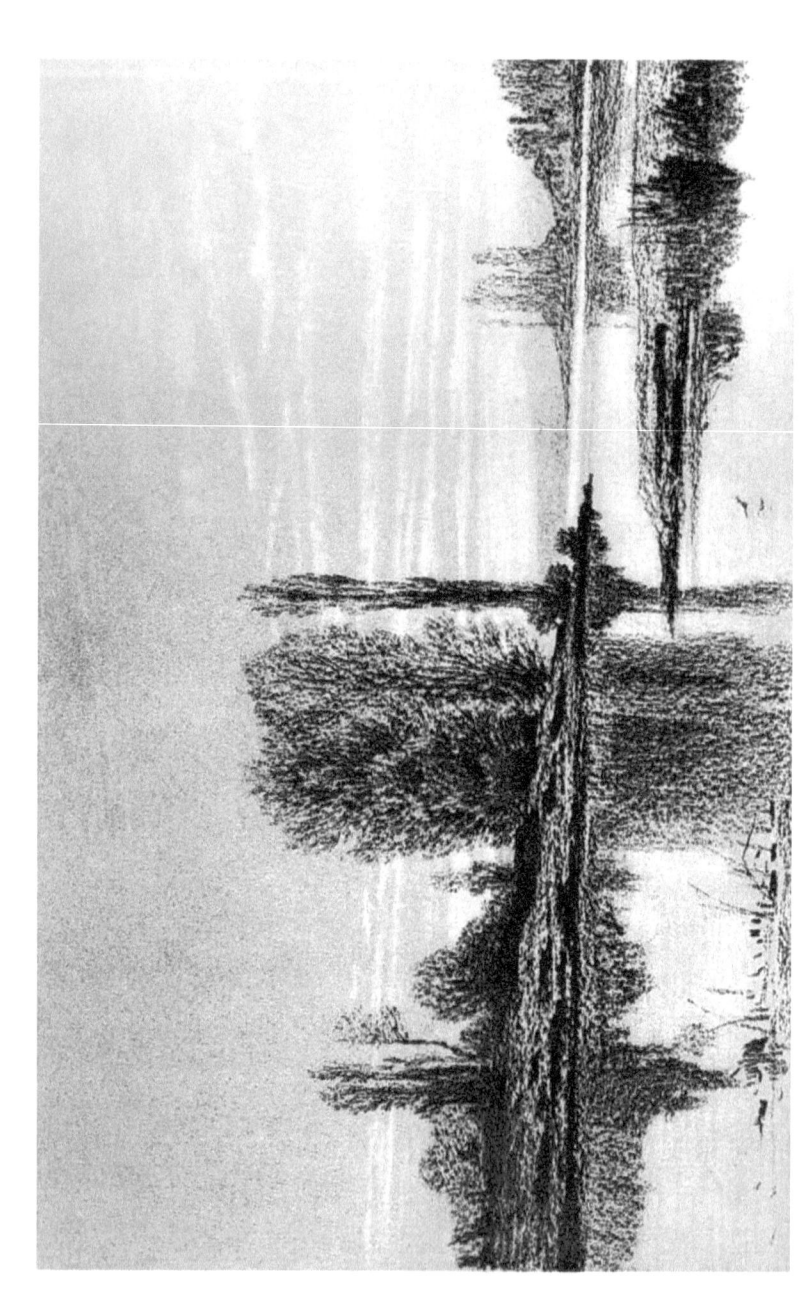

WRITTEN LESSONS.

LESSON FIRST.

SOUVENIR D'AUVERS.

Now, reader, that you understand all the accessories that you have to employ, we are going to do our best to teach you the use of them, by practicing together, if you are willing. The first drawing that we submit to you. Souvenir D'Auvers (PL. No. 2), is simple in execution; for that reason we have chosen it for our first lesson.*

---

* You can obtain in Paris, at the shop of M. G. Meusnier, rue Neuve-Saint-Augustin, No. 27, the plate

In the first place, you must take the outside measure of your drawing, making four
lines, very light because they are not to remain; then, when you have the size of your
work, with your charcoal crayon cut or worn
flat and a little broad, pass a general tone
from left to right, beginning at the top, and
that in the most regular manner possible
and so that there shall remain no white
spaces between your touches in any direction. The paper once covered, by the aid of
your four fingers joined, or, better still (because this sky tone is very clear), by the help
of your rag, spread your charcoal, turning
from the right to the left and beginning at the
bottom, in order that the rag, gathering more
charcoal from the lower part, may leave you a
more vigorous tone at the top, which will

(Souvenir d'Auvers) of the size of the original, about
14 x 11 inches, and also a collection of models and
progressive studies, either by hiring them or by sub-
scription.

make your sky fall back and give it the desired perspective. You have thus your background, sky and water. With some bread-
crumb you must take off all that passes the
limits of your drawing, lines which should
already disappear under the work of the rag;
then you must take the measure of your
drawing again, this time without making
lines, for nature has no outlines and Charcoal
Drawing permits you to give form only by
masses, shadows and lights.

On the background which you have already
laid, you make your sketch; that is to say,
you mark your masses lightly to obtain their
position, which you must rectify until it is
very exact. For your first trials, take mea-
surements if you find them necessary; but,
when you have a little more practice, your
eye ought to guide you, and, to obtain the
position and size of your objects, you will
simply compare one with another. Thus, in
the design which we are studying, you see

that the ground from the left to the right is
at about one-third of the whole height, starting from the bottom of the drawing, and that
it grows gradually narrower toward the right;
you will indicate it by massing it with a flat
and vigorous tone. You mass, then, your
background much more lightly and rub it in
with the stomp. The first plane is a piece of
ground which is about half way between your
horizon and the bottom of your drawing; you
mass it in the same manner as your ground in
your second plane, but less vigorously in
the upper part, and by passing your crayon
lightly over it, so as to obtain that grain
which you observe in your model. Then
you see that the middle of your drawing
is occupied by the group of willows which
are in the strongest shadow; indicate this
group, observing that its width is about two-
thirds of its height, and place the little poplar
on the right, at its proper distance.

Then take the middle point between this

poplar and the right extremity of the drawing, where you will place the group of poplars
in the background, and then draw all the details which are on the right and on the left
of this mass. After this, make the reflections in the water. And here we wish you to
notice that the general tone of the water is,
as in nature, a little more vigorous than the
tone of the sky; to obtain it, pass over, with
your crayon, a light tone which you will
spread with your finger. The reflections
ought to be sketched very perpendicular and
in a general vigorous tone.

Here is, then, the sketching out and the
putting in position of your drawing. Try to
be exact, especially in your first attempts,
otherwise you will come to content yourself
with being nearly right, which is a fatal weak-
ness. It is very well, however, when you begin, to mass a little under the model; that is
to say, make your objects a little smaller, very
little, the tenth of an inch perhaps, in this

case, so that, afterwards, in working out the details you may reach the exact measure of your model; otherwise you gain a little in spite of yourself and make your object too large. Your drawing then loses in elegance.

For the details in the execution, we proceed in the same order as for the sketching. The sky is so simple that we need not enlarge upon it; there is nothing to do but to mark out the white spots forming clouds, with bread-crumb. A light touch with the stomp will indicate the little cloud at the top of the drawing on the right.

Next, we shall attack the ground on the second plane, where we find the principal *motif* of the design, and for this we begin by drawing the line of demarkation between the land and the water; speaking artistically, establish the vigors which arrest the land at the edge of the water. Then, if the general tone is correct, draw with the crayon every vigorous detail as exactly as possible and, with bread-crumb already a little soiled, we lighten the luminous parts of the half-tint. Take notice that we say the bread-crumb ought to be a little soiled ; this is important, otherwise we shall have the same light as in the sky or on the brilliant parts of the water.

The ground being finished, you will proceed with each detail upon it, drawing with the crayon well sharpened and lighting them up with the spill or with the stomp, taking care that the vigorous details, fence, branches, etc., be very clearly and carefully placed and. that the background be lighter than the bright spots on the land itself.

The working of the group of willows in the middle is very simple. It is made of two vigorous tones lightened on each side by the spills ; in the middle you may use the eraser to take out some details of the leaf.

Here we may remark that, in employing the eraser, it is convenient to hold it in a particular manner. Let the handle of the eraser be under the hand, in such way that you can perceive only the blade and the end of the handle. This is the way it is held by clerks when they want to erase a large blot.

To return to our drawing; take out with bread-crumb the clean lights which separate the branches of the tree on the right of the group. This done, draw the middle poplar very perpendicular, in working up the charcoal with a slender and close-twisted spill.

The poplars in the background on the right, should be modeled with the stomp or, better still, you can indicate with it the general mass well rubbed in and then cut out the form or the profile with bread-crumb. Then you may draw the ground on the first plane as you did that on the left, taking care to make it detach itself well from the water which it divides; but do this without making any lines, solely by the opposition of lights and of vigors.

The drawing may be finished by the exe-

cution of the water. Permit me, reader, to
repeat here what I said above ; give great
care to your water, that is the great charm
of Charcoal Drawing. A Charcoal Drawing without water is like "a book without
a preface or a man who goes out without a
hat ;" consult a hundred amateurs, ninety-nine
will tell you that your drawing lacks some-
thing. Therefore you can not treat this ele-
ment of success with too much care. You
may employ every means to render the trans-
parency and the reflection of the water ; paper
stomps, leather stomps, cork, wadding, etc.
Nothing, in our opinion, is better than the
pith of the elder, cut flat. In our drawing
you can spread the charcoal with the elder
pith very regularly, taking care that the
touches melt well together as if they were all
made with one single stroke. Then give the
vigors which reflect the masses in the shadow,
and by caressing the charcoal with the edge
of the eraser you have the half tints.

Last of all, you will give the brilliant touches of sunlight which just strike the surface of the water, with the edge of a ball of bread-crumb very carefully flattened. When your drawing is finished, set it as we have shown you above.

LESSON SECOND.

THE BROOK (SOUVENIR OF NORMANDY)*.

You may have remarked, in sketching the first plate, that the backgrounds are worked up at once with a spill or a paper stomp ; you should proceed in the same way with the brook. After having passed over your paper a general tone for the sky with a rag covered with charcoal dust, you must model the poplars in the back ground with a spill, first massing them very lightly with the crayon ; then commence your positions at the left, taking care to denote the very delicate contours in the drawing.

The land, sketched as we have told you

* see frontispiece

above, will then be worked up with the stomp
and retouched with bread-crumb on the road
that leads to the fence. The piece of ground
which forms the bank at the right, is rubbed
in only in spots and is modeled by the crayon
itself. The water should be treated as in
the other study. You see that we can give
very few instructions on the manner of treating this second drawing, since every design
contains all the proceedings applied to Charcoal Drawing. There is nothing to be found
here which we have not indicated above. It is
quite enough, then, for serious study, to copy
some good models and to notice well the
manner in which the artist avails himself of
his means. For this, the half-tint obtained by
the eraser is easily recognized; let it be the
line of the water or a reed, its form is always
clear and distinct; the bread-crumb, on the
contrary, gives a broader and more brilliant
form; and in the half-tints made by the spill,
you can obtain your lights with the leather

stomp, if you wish, often less bright than with the bread-crumb.

What we have just said, contradicts that prejudice which many artists have against Charcoal Drawing, which they say is only a tissue of tricks. There are but few means; in this work we do not seek to hide the fact; but the artist must study seriously the mode of employing them, if he wishes to give just values, which is the basis of painting and above all of landscape painting.

GENBEAL LESSON,

OR MANNER OP TREATING ANY SUBJECT.

There is no landscape, however extended it may be, which embraces, in itself alone, all that nature can present. Therefore, the preceding lessons and the models chosen have for their object only to designate the methods employed for those different subjects.

If we had to explain the manner of rendering every landscape, ten volumes and a hundred plates would not be enough.

We shall try, in this chapter, to guide the amateur and to give him the fullest instructions possible, so that, through whatever country he may travel, he will not be embarrassed in filling his album with souvenirs.

The Sky.

If you have to render a blue and clear sky, as in summer, treat it simply with the rag, as we have described above; if it is of an intense blue, as in winter in frosty weather, work it up with the thumb or with the palm of the hand, this will leave it the vigor it ought to have.

Apropos to this, we find a very interesting paragraph in the pamphlet of M. Armand Chamey, which is worth quoting: "If you have a sky of clear blue or of luminous white, be careful not to cover your paper with a uniform tint. The orientalists, who have brought back to us landscapes resembling Chinese shadows pasted on a background of uniform blue, have fallen into a profound error in ima-

gining that they can render thus the depth
and intensity of the southern skies. Decamps
and Delacroix have always avoided this
fault—they are observers too clear sighted to
fall into it. The purest sky is never uniform; if you look at it fixedly, you will see
myriads of spots of a blue more or less deep,
which have the appearance of moving. It is
this resonance, this vibration of the light
which you should try to render; without it
there is no air, no space, no depth in the picture. A light tint rubbed over with cotton,
which you can work up by breaking it into
luminous points with bread-crumb, renders
very well the effect of which we have just
spoken, but you will be very far from succeed-
ing in this always. Therefore it is better to
choose generally cloudy skies, which exact
much less care and trouble."

To render an effect of storm, a cloudy sky,
model your clouds with the stomp or the
leather, always in the direction in which they

are moving; lighten them with bread-crmnb if you wish to obtain those brilliant sunlight effects which every-where gild the sky before or after a storm.

But above all, let your tone of background or of azure be always very smooth, and let your clouds detach themselves well, that is what will give depth and movement to your sky.

The Water.

Water presents itself under many aspects; sleeping, as in a lake, a pool, etc., it always reflects the objects which border it or which are near to it. But the running water of rivers does not always reflect these objects, or else it presents their image in a thousand different ways.

At sunrise the reflection is, so to say, flat

and without brilliancy. At noon, scarcely any reflection; the water is very brilliant, sometimes it is even brighter than the sky.

It is in the evening, from four o'clock till sunset, that water presents itself in the manner most charming for the artist. The reflections then are clear and calm and reproduce objects as in a mirror, in all their values and their varieties of tone. For this you must use all the resources of Charcoal Drawing—elder-pith, leather stomps, eraser; you must avail yourself of them all if you wish to succeed in rendering the variety of nature.

The Ground.

It is not, accurately speaking, the ground itself which ofifers serious difficulties of execution, but what the soil bears: shrubs.

plants, rocks, etc. It is especially diflficult to
carry these details over the ground so as to
make them a part of it and cause you to feel
that the one produces the other. To succeed
in this, you must establish well the ground
tone of your soil, and for this take care not to
leave any of the white of the paper; you
should use that only when you want a bright
sunlight on a rocky ground; for however
light grass and other details of the sort may
be, they are far from the brilliancy of sunlight on a white house or on a stone. It is
well to be very moderate in the use of this
brilliant tone, which, when employed, gives an
excellent result even when it exaggerates the
effect.

The Trees.

One of the most troublesome tasks of the amateur is the execution of foliage. And yet it is very difficult to give absolute rules for this work, for at a certain distance, such a distance as that at which the student generally places himself to get a view, the details of the foliage disappear completely; the masses alone are visible. To know how to lighten these masses and to maintain them on the shadow, there the study of foliage ought to end, and working after nature is really the only means of acquiring that knowledge. It is in the study of foliage above all that almost all the methods of teaching known at this day are defective. For, I repeat, unless you have your tree completely in the foreground, you should not occupy yourself with the foliage, and even in that case you should make its quality felt only by the touch and not by drawing it leaf by leaf. But if, on the second plane, you wish to indicate the foliage in a mass, either lightened or in half-tint, then the eraser will be very useful to you, by employing it simply in the direction of the leaf, which will give its form, and by bearing on more or less forcibly, which will give you a variety of lights that you can render more brilliant with bread-crumb.

You may use also a paint-brush, more or less moistened, or even dry, but this ought to be employed only in great moderation. This process, if it is not practiced with the greatest skill, gives a monotonous stippling which is not in harmony with the rest of the drawing.

Buildings.

Offer no serious difficulty. You can easily obtain their perspective by their relation to the objects which surround them. There is no need of making a special study of perspective. It is well, in general, to treat buildings largely, and for that, close your eyes slightly, so as to see only the salient details.

Mountains.

The sharp and picturesque sites of Switzerland and of the Pyrenees, so frequented by tourists, are well suited to Charcoal

Drawing, because of the quickness with which it seizes the effects always so fugitive among mountains. You should distrust all harsh lines in the treatment of such subjects, above all in backgrounds where the profiles of the mountains cross each other on different planes. For the rest, mountains ought to be treated with the same vigor and with the same solidity as the ground.

The Rocks and the Sea; the Sands.

Which of you, my readers, has not seen those fine drawings of the sea-shore, by Allongé, the Souvenirs of Brittany, with their dolmens and their men-hirs, in the midst of that severe and almost savage nature? And those coasts of Normandy, where the master excels in rendering the low tide sands when the water has gone out of sight?

You may easily succeed in rendering the sea-shore itself, but you need serious study to render the atmosphere and its immensity, and above all to vary your drawings from nature. I need not repeat here that rocks and cliffs should be solid and vigorous, but there needs very different work for the sky, the sea and the sand. The sea should generally be rendered by the paper stomp and with a tolerably vigorous tone, the foam of the waves by bread-crumb. The sand is to be treated by the thumb or, if you wish to obtain the grain of the wet sand lighted up by the sun, here you may make use of that process spoken of by various artists; that is, to draw your charcoal crayon lightly over your paper, so that the grain may catch the friable particles of the charcoal, and let the white of the paper be seen between the interstices.

And now, reader, permit me to close this chapter by recommending to you again variety in your work. This is an important point, and for want of taking account of it, many amateurs, artists even, fall into monotony and uniformity, defects for which no genius can compensate, especially in artistic work.

SKETCHES IN CHARCOAL.

Sketches in charcoal ought to render only effects. You make a sketch only when you want to catch a passing effect, or when time presses and does not permit, you to make a careful drawing from nature. Look at the plate entitled Sunlight in the Woods. How well Charcoal Drawing, even when rapidly executed, can render this impression of nature! We can not undertake to show how such sketches are made; it is there especially that skill makes itself seen. In our model, the background is a rough surface smoothed over by the thumb, the ground worked down by the stomp, then, the trees once drawn and the masses put in place, the artist obtained his sunlight effects by bread-crumb. We believe that it would be very useful, after having made serious studies from nature, to make some of these sketches, rapidly drawn. In this way you can keep a great number of impressions and remembrances of nature.

ON RETOUCHING

AFTER THE FIXING OF THE DRAWING.

Charcoal Drawing is minute work from
this point of view, that it sometimes happens that, after having fixed your work, you
find it incomplete from want of vigor in the
first planes, or else it is too dry because you
have kept it on a scale of tones much too
dark. This latter trouble happens more frequently than the former, because the fixative
always darkens the drawing perceptibly, and
if you make your general tone only slightly
vigorous, it is lost in blackness after the
fixing. To obviate this inconvenience, which,
however, will not present itself after some

study and practice, you may advantageously use the rubber crayon, especially to lighten the background.

If, on the other hand, the drawing fails for want of solidity or of vigor, you can repeat certain touches with a very black charcoal crayon, such as the natural branch or twig well charred, or even the black crayon Conté.

These vigorous retouches made, you can fix them by the help of the atomizer, or fix the whole drawing again ; otherwise, if you fix these touches only by the ordinary means, the fixative laid on a second time will form a circle over the first and make a spot.

You may also work up a Charcoal Drawing by means of *gouache*,* of white crayons or by some touches of oil, to obtain very brilliant lights ; but you should use these

* *Gouache*—water colors mixed with gum-water.

means very scrupulously. If you employ oil colors, mix a little cadmium or yellow ochre with the silver white, which will give a tone at once warm and very luminous. If you have been so imprudent as to make a sketch without having prepared your sky tone, you may still obtain it, even after fixing your work, by the help of your linen roll dipped into charcoal dust, which you can pass lightly over your drawing. This will not give a great delicacy, but it will take away the crudity of the drawing, especially if it is made on white paper.

STUDY FROM NATURE.

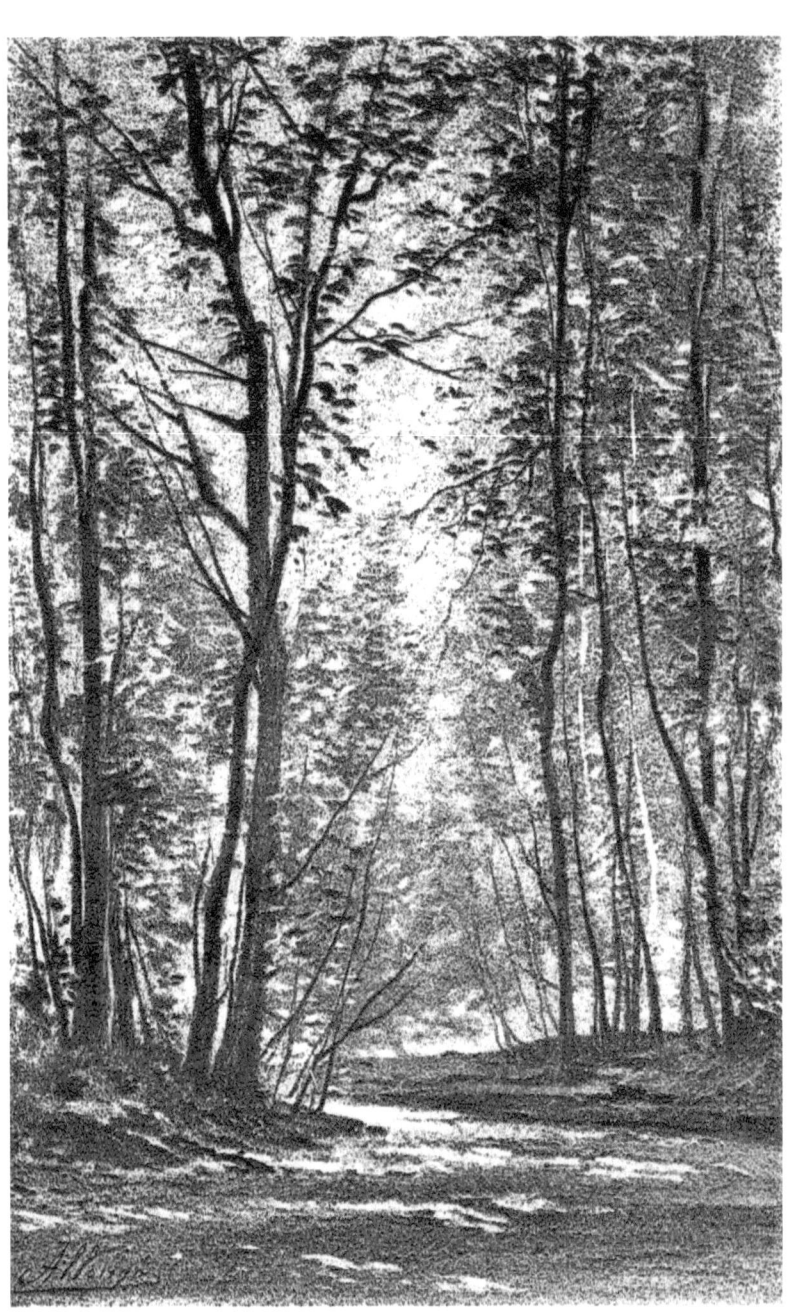

STUDY FROM NATURE.

CONCLUSION.

It is now, reader, that you must endeavor to be yourself and try to make yourself original. For that, forget, before nature, what you have copied ; do not try to draw like this or that artist, but simply draw what you see.

The manner of working alone ought to remain with you, so that, your *motif* once chosen, the execution will not embarrass you.

The first time that you work from nature,

choose a quiet subject, the corner of a wood, a
glimpse of a river or of a field. Avoid
space, extent, in a word all complex landscape.
That will come later, but take care not to go
too quickly, I know very well that the great
desire of an amateur, when he goes to the
country, is to bring back complete little landscapes, which can be framed. But, I repeat
it, a little patience, and instead of having
a gallery of your works you will have, it is
true, only a few drawings, but these will easily
find their admirers.

The first studies ought to be studies of
trees ; the tree, it has been said, is the academy of landscape ; nothing is more true, and
he who knows how to draw a tree well, that is
to say, to construct it well and to lighten up
its masses, will find no difficulty when he
attempts a whole landscape. Water, sky,
buildings, all present their difficulties it is true,
but the tree is and always will be the serious
difficulty in landscape, since it is the study

which gives back the least result from skill
in work or from good methods, A few buildings drawn with care, you have them all; a
few borders of the water carefully studied,
your waters will always be transparent, and
your skies will leave nothing to desire if you
begin by treating them simply.

But every tree bears in itself its mark
of originality; the oak has a thousand ways
of being broad and powerful; the supple
and elegant poplar, the willow, the elm, the
aspen, the plane-tree change, a thousand
times, their form and aspect, from one season to another. Therefore they must be
studied with the greatest care; watch them
even when they put on certain bizarre forms,
if you wish to understand them well, and
never forget that you must always build up
your tree, no matter how lightly, before
marking out its masses, or putting in its effects. In recalling your last lesson, vou will
remember that each object ought to be ren-

dered differently, this always happens in nature. The trees themselves ought to be treated after their kind. Render the willow by light rubbings; the oak with vigorous, nay, brutal, masses; the poplar with energy in touch, for it is a tree of strong tonality, but give to this touch the delicacy and the suppleness which characterize the poplar.

I will not go back upon each detail. Try above all to make your drawing harmonize in all its parts, and after some months of study from nature, you will arrive at the best results, as I promised you in the beginning of this book; nay more, at better results than you can have hoped for in the beginning.

Here, dear reader, is the summing up of all the instruction that I have received and that I transmit to you. May it make of you what it has made of me, an amateur, a lover and an admirer of Charcoal Drawing and of its artists.

TABLE OF CONTENTS.

STUDIES AND LESSONS.

www.ingramcontent.com/pod-product-compliance
Lightning Source LLC
Chambersburg PA
CBHW030713220526
45463CB00005B/2032